Passive Income

Through

NFT

A Beginners Guide To Non-Fungible Token

S.P. MODI

Disclaimer Notice

The content of this book is concerned with generating a passive income stream through Non-Fungible Token (NFS), which is the second most searched topic around the world after crypto currencies. One thing to know is that each token has its own or distinct value, which may or may not be similar, copied, or followed by another token. Cultural variations can influence the value of crypto currency. Investors must have a wider vision, which necessitates certain traits that aid them in making sound choices in order to pick the right tokens and build their own diversified financial portfolio. This author and or rights owner(s) make no claims, promises, or guarantees in regard to the accuracy, completeness, or adequacy of the contents of this book, and expressly disclaims liability for errors and omissions in the contents within. Picking-up the right token, and/or right wallet to transact in crypto currencies is an art or a skill that one needs to identify and develop over a course of time, or one can follow the advice of the subject matter expert to build a profitable portfolio of diversified crypto currencies and tokens. No warranties of any kind are declared or implied. By reading this book, the reader agrees that under no circumstances is the author responsible for any losses, direct or indirect, which are incurred as a result of the use of the information contained in this book, including but not limited to any inaccuracies or typo mistakes.

Copyright Notice

Cover credit

I am sincerely thankful to Marmie S. for her creative vision in designing the beautiful & eye catchy covers for all my books.

Instagram ID: mi29creations

Index

CHAPTER 1

Introduction to Non-Fungible Token

First of all, let's us accept that cryptocurrency is an intangible currency and can't be physically touched like our traditional currencies. In other words, Cryptocurrency is a digital or virtual currency that utilizes encryption techniques to secure transactions and to regulate the generation of new units. It operates independently of a central bank and is decentralized, which means that it is not subject to the traditional financial regulatory framework that applies to traditional currencies. It is essentially a form of digital money that allows for the exchange of goods and services in a peer-to-peer manner without the need for intermediaries such as banks, hence it will save your excess funds on transaction fees.

In recent years, the cryptocurrency industry has grown exponentially, revolutionizing the way people invest and use digital assets. Now, a new concept is gaining traction: Non-Fungible Tokens (NFTs). NFTs are unique digital assets that are created on the blockchain and cannot be replicated or exchanged. They represent ownership of digital items such as art, music, and games, and are fast becoming the go-to solution for creating and trading digital assets.

In this book, we will explore how NFTs are taking over the digital world and what it means for the future of cryptocurrency. Non-Fungible Tokens (NFTs) are emerging as a revolutionary solution to the problem of digital ownership. NFTs, unlike traditional cryptocurrencies, represent a unique digital asset on a blockchain that cannot be replicated or exchanged, making them perfect for verifying digital ownership. NFTs are quickly gaining momentum, especially in the digital art world, where they allow artists to monetize their digital works, which would otherwise be prone to theft and piracy. Apart from digital art, NFTs are also finding their way into other industries, such as music and gaming. In music, artists can create unique digital album covers, which can then be sold as NFTs, allowing fans to own a piece of their favorite artist's work.

Similarly, gaming companies are using NFTs to create rare in-game items that can be traded and owned by players. With the rising popularity of NFTs, it is clear that they are here to stay and could soon be a standard in the digital world.

What are Non-Fungible Tokens (NFTs)?

The concept of Non-Fungible Tokens (NFTs) may seem confusing at first, but once you understand the basics, you'll realize just how revolutionary they are. NFTs are unique digital assets that are created on the blockchain, the same technology that powers cryptocurrencies like Bitcoin and Ethereum. Unlike cryptocurrencies, however, NFTs cannot be exchanged or replicated.

In simple words, NFTs represent ownership of a specific digital item, whether it's a piece of art, a song, a video, or even virtual real estate. Each NFT is distinct and has its own value, making it impossible to interchange them like you would with cryptocurrencies. This uniqueness is what sets NFTs apart and makes them so appealing to digital creators and collectors.

Now, you might be thinking, how exactly do NFTs work?

Well, at the core of every NFT is a smart contract, which is a self-executing contract with the terms of the agreement directly written into the code. These smart contracts contain all the necessary information about the digital asset, such as its title, description, and ownership details. When someone purchases an NFT, the ownership rights are transferred to their digital wallet, recorded on the blockchain for everyone to see.

One of the major benefits of NFTs is the ability to prove authenticity and ownership. In the past, digital artists and creators struggled to protect their work from being copied or stolen online. With NFTs, artists can mint their work as an NFT, creating a digital certificate of authenticity that is unique and verifiable. This gives creators more control over their digital assets and ensures that they are properly credited and compensated for their digital work.

Additionally, NFTs provide new avenues for monetization for digital creators. By selling their work as NFTs, artists can earn royalties whenever their NFT is resold on secondary markets. This creates a recurring revenue stream for artists and allows them to profit from the increasing value of their digital creations.

NFT's Inception

Have you heard of Non-Fungible Tokens (NFTs)? If not, you're not alone. NFTs are only beginning to gain attention in the digital world, but they have been around since 2014 when the first NFT was sold by the now popular blockchain game, Cryptokitties. However, it wasn't until 2020 that NFTs began to make headlines with crypto-collectibles, digital art, and a range of other applications like sports memorabilia. Now, everyone is wondering what NFTs are and how they're taking over the digital world.

In other words, NFTs are a form of cryptocurrency that represents a unique digital asset, whether it be artwork, music, videos, or even tweets. The concept of NFTs is simple - they give the ownership and authenticity of digital assets to the buyer. This means that the creator can sell their digital asset to a collector, and that collector can own the unique version of that asset. The value of NFTs depends on the demand for the digital asset they represent and can be sold for millions of dollars. The use cases for NFTs are expanding, with many artists and musicians leveraging the technology to sell their work directly to consumers. They're also being used for ticketing, gaming, and even virtual real estate. NFTs are revolutionizing the way people view digital ownership and are rapidly changing the digital space. While technology is still in its infancy, it's expected to become more mainstream in the coming years. NFTs are no longer a niche concept, they're becoming a crucial part of the future of digital ownership.

In the next few chapters, we'll explain exactly what NFTs are and how they're impacting the digital space. So, if you're looking to learn more about NFTs and how they're changing the digital world, then read on!

Allow me to simplify the concept of NFTs:

If you're an absolute beginner looking to understand NFT, the concept can be quite intimidating and confusing at first but once you understand the basics, you'll realize just how revolutionary they are. Here is a simplified version of what it means and how it works.

NFTs are unique digital assets that are created on the blockchain, the same technology that powers cryptocurrencies like Bitcoin and Ethereum. Unlike cryptocurrencies, however, NFTs cannot be exchanged or replicated.

In other words, NFTs represent ownership of a specific digital item, whether it's a piece of art, a song, a video, or even virtual real estate. Each NFT is distinct and has its own value, making it impossible to interchange them like you would with cryptocurrencies. This uniqueness is what sets NFTs apart and makes them so appealing to digital creators and collectors.

But how exactly do NFTs work? Well, at the core of every NFT is a smart contract, which is a self-executing contract with the terms of the agreement directly written into the code. These smart contracts contain all the necessary information about the digital asset, such as its title, description, and ownership details. When someone purchases an NFT, the ownership rights are transferred to their digital wallet, recorded on the blockchain for everyone to see.

One of the major benefits of NFTs is the ability to prove authenticity and ownership. In the past, digital artists and creators struggled to protect their work from being copied or stolen online. With NFTs, artists can mint their work as an NFT, creating a digital certificate of authenticity that is unique and verifiable. This gives creators more control over their digital assets and ensures that they are properly credited and compensated for their work.

Furthermore, NFTs provide new avenues for monetization for digital creators. By selling their work as NFTs, artists can earn royalties whenever their NFT is resold on secondary markets. This creates a recurring revenue stream for artists and allows them to profit from the increasing value of their digital creations.

You might be thinking, 'what differentiates digital NFTs and Cryptocurrencies?'

As the world has evolved into a global digital village, so has the need for digital currencies. Cryptocurrencies and Non-Fungible Tokens (NFTs) are both digital assets that are created on the blockchain, but there are some key differences between the two.

First and foremost, the main difference lies in their fungibility. Cryptocurrencies like Bitcoin and Ethereum are fungible, meaning that each individual unit of the currency is interchangeable with any other unit of the same value. For example, one Bitcoin is the same as any other Bitcoin. This is similar to traditional currencies like the US dollar or the Euro, or the UK pound, where each unit of currency is identical and can be exchanged freely.

Whereas, on the other hand, NFTs are non-fungible, meaning that each NFT is unique and cannot be exchanged on a one-to-one basis with another NFT. Each NFT represents ownership of a specific digital item, whether it's a piece of art, music, or a virtual item. This uniqueness is what sets NFTs apart and gives them their value. While cryptocurrencies can be used as a medium of exchange, NFTs are primarily used to represent ownership and provenance of digital assets.

Another major difference I can point here between cryptocurrencies and NFTs is their purpose. Cryptocurrencies were created as a decentralized form of digital currency that can be used for financial transactions, just like traditional currencies. They serve as a store of value, a medium of exchange, and a unit of account. On the other hand, NFTs were created to represent ownership of digital assets and provide a way for digital creators to monetize their work. NFTs have opened up a whole new world of possibilities for artists, musicians, and creators, allowing them to sell their work directly to collectors and earn royalties on secondary sales.

Additionally, the value of cryptocurrencies is determined by factors such as supply and demand, market speculation, and the underlying technology. NFTs, on the other hand, derive their value from the perceived value of the digital asset they represent. The value of an NFT is often influenced by factors such as the popularity and reputation of the creator, the uniqueness of the asset, and the demand from collectors.

And how do NFTs work?

NFTs may seem like a complex concept, but once you understand how they work, you'll see just how innovative and exciting they are. At the core of every NFT is a smart contract, which is a self-executing contract with the terms of the agreement directly written into the code. These smart contracts contain all the necessary information about the digital asset, such as its title, description, and ownership details. When someone purchases an NFT, the ownership rights are transferred to their digital wallet, recorded on the blockchain for everyone to see.

But what does it mean to own an NFT? Owning an NFT means that you have a digital certificate of ownership for a specific digital item. This could be a piece of digital art, a music track, a video clip, or even virtual real estate. The unique code of the NFT ensures that it cannot be duplicated or tampered with, providing a level of authenticity and provenance that is unparalleled in the digital world.

The value of an NFT is determined by various factors. The popularity and reputation of the creator play a significant role in determining the value of an NFT. The uniqueness and scarcity of the digital item also contribute to its value. Additionally, the demand from collectors and investors can drive up the price of an NFT. It's important to note that the value of an NFT can fluctuate over time, just like any other asset. This means that owning an NFT can be a speculative investment, with the potential for both gains and losses.

Once you own an NFT, you have several options. You can choose to display your NFT in a digital gallery or virtual museum, showcasing your ownership of a unique piece of digital art. You can also trade or sell your NFT on various NFT marketplaces, allowing you to monetize your investment or pass it on to another collector. Some NFTs even come with additional perks, such as exclusive access to events or merchandise.

In summary, NFTs are unique digital assets that are created on the blockchain using smart contracts. They represent ownership of a specific digital item and provide a level of authenticity and provenance that is revolutionizing the digital world. Whether you're a digital creator looking to monetize your work or a collector looking to invest in unique digital assets, NFTs offer endless possibilities and are reshaping the future of digital ownership.

Now, you might be thinking, 'Benefits of NFTs for Digital Creators?'

Digital creators have long struggled to monetize their work in the digital realm, with piracy and copyright infringement running rampant. However, Non-Fungible Tokens (NFTs) are changing the game for digital creators, offering a range of benefits that were previously unimaginable.

One of the key benefits of NFTs for digital creators is the ability to prove authenticity and ownership. By minting their work as an NFT, creators can establish a digital certificate of authenticity that is unique and verifiable. This not only protects their work from being copied or stolen, but it also ensures that they receive proper credit and compensation for their creations. This newfound control over their intellectual property empowers digital creators to confidently share and distribute their work, knowing that they will be properly recognized and rewarded.

Additionally, NFTs provide a new stream of revenue for digital creators. When they sell their work as an NFT, they can earn royalties on secondary sales. This means that if their NFT is resold on a secondary marketplace, the creator will receive a percentage of the sale. This creates a recurring revenue stream for digital creators, allowing them to continue to profit from the increasing value of their creations over time. This has the potential to be particularly lucrative for artists, musicians, and other creators whose work is highly sought after by collectors.

Moreover, NFTs can also be used as a tool for social impact. Some digital creators are using their NFTs to raise funds for charitable causes, while others are using them to support underrepresented communities or promote environmental sustainability. This creates a new way for creators to leverage their talent and reach a wider audience, while also making a positive difference in the world. By using NFTs for social good, digital creators are able to not only monetize their work but also create meaningful impact and bring attention to important causes.

CHAPTER 2

Understanding NFT Technology

As we have observed, the world is in a continuous state of change and the introduction of blockchain technology is one of the latest innovative advancements that has revolutionized various industries. This new technological phenomenon has gained immense attention over the last decade and is slowly becoming an essential building block of our digital world. The discussion on this technology has reached every corner and is surely gaining more interest from people after learning of Bitcoin's market value. Blockchain is a distributed ledger system that is decentralized and transparent, so it is free from all the middleman in other words, banks. It's one of the latest and most exciting innovations in the digital world and is fast transforming the way we exchange and record information.

Let's take a precise look at the core technology behind **Non-Fungible Tokens (NFTs)** and how it functions.

Understanding the core technology behind Non-Fungible Tokens (NFTs) is essential to grasp their true potential and impact in the digital world. NFTs are built on blockchain technology, which is the same technology that powers cryptocurrencies like Bitcoin and Ethereum. Blockchain is a decentralized ledger that records transactions in a transparent and secure manner.

The core functionality of NFTs lies in their ability to create unique digital assets and establish ownership and provenance. Each NFT is represented by a smart contract, a self-executing contract with the terms of the agreement directly written into the code. These smart contracts contain all the necessary information about the digital asset, including its title, description, and ownership details.

The technology behind NFTs ensures that each token is unique and cannot be replicated or tampered with. This is achieved through cryptographic algorithms and the use of metadata that is stored on the blockchain. The metadata contains information about the asset, such as its creator, date of creation, and any additional attributes.

In simple terms, NFT technology enables the creation of a digital certificate of ownership for a specific digital item. It ensures that the ownership rights are securely recorded on the blockchain, providing transparency and immutability. This technology has revolutionized the way digital assets are valued, traded, and protected.

As NFT technology continues to evolve, we can expect to see further advancements and innovations that will shape the future of digital ownership and creative expression. The possibilities are endless, and NFTs are just the beginning of a new era in digital space.

What is Blockchain?

The concept of blockchain can be understood by its name itself. A blockchain is a block of data that is stored in a chain. Chain in other words can be understood as a connecting line of blocks. Each block in the chain contains various information such as the previous block's data and its own. Once a block has been added to the chain, it cannot be changed. The chain of blocks acts as a ledger where all the data and transactions are recorded. Blockchain was created to allow secure and transparent transactions, and as such, it has become the new digital currency of the world.

How does blockchain function and operate?

Technically, a blockchain system comprises three critical elements: Nodes, Miners, and Cryptography. The system works in a distributed manner, meaning that there is no central entity that manages the information stored in the blocks. Instead, each node in the network has a copy of the ledger, and all nodes can verify the transactions. Cryptography ensures the security of data within the network. Each block in a blockchain has two important components, the header and the body. The header contains the hash of the previous block, the nonce, and a timestamp. The body contains the transaction data and other relevant information. Once a block is mined, its hash is added to the header of the next block, which ensures that the blockchain is immutable. In essence, this creates a chain of blocks, hence the name blockchain.

What are Nodes?

Nodes refer to individual computers that have joined the blockchain network. They play a crucial role in maintaining and validating the data stored in the blockchain. All the nodes within the network contain a copy of the ledger, and whenever a new transaction is recorded, the information is propagated to every node in the network. Each node validates and confirms the transaction using specific rules and algorithms. In other words, nodes serve as validators and make it possible for every user in the blockchain network to access and interact with the ledger.

What are Miners?

The miners are essential actors in the blockchain system as they are responsible for creating new blocks and adding them to the blockchain. A miner's work is to validate transactions by verifying them, then adding them to the blockchain. After completing a set of transactions, miners combine them into a block, and to create a new block, the miners must solve a cryptographic puzzle. The solution to the puzzle (nonce) serves as a proof-of-work, which provides the blockchain network with security and transparency.

Therefore, to conclude, Blockchain is a type of technology that stores information or data in a secure and decentralized manner. Imagine it as a digital ledger, similar to a book, but with some amazing features added to it. Once information is recorded on the blockchain, it cannot be changed or deleted, making it immutable and trustworthy. It works by using complex algorithms to create a digital fingerprint or hash for every piece of data added to the network, ensuring its authenticity. The beauty of the blockchain is that it operates without a central authority or intermediary (such as banks), making it transparent and democratic. Every user in the network has a copy of the blockchain and verifies all transactions. In short, blockchain is a new and innovative way of storing and sharing data that offers unmatched security, transparency, and immutability.

CHAPTER 3

Types of Non-Fungible Tokens (NFTs)

As the world has grown increasingly dependent on digital systems after the internet revolution and smart phone revolution, new methods of exchanging currency have rapidly arisen, giving way to a whole new world of cryptocurrencies and NFTs.

NFTs have taken the digital world by storm, and there are already several popular examples of NFTs that have made headlines and captured the attention of collectors and enthusiasts.

Below are just a few of the most notable examples of NFTs in use today:

1. "Everydays:
The First 5000 Days" by Beeple:

This NFT artwork made history when it sold at auction for a staggering $69 million. Created by digital artist Beeple, the artwork is a collage of his daily creations spanning over 5,000 days. This sale catapulted NFT art into the mainstream and demonstrated the incredible value that can be achieved in the NFT market.

2. NBA Top Shot:

This NFT platform allows basketball fans to collect and trade officially licensed NBA highlight videos. Each video clip is minted as an NFT and can be bought, sold, and traded on the platform. NBA Top Shot has gained massive popularity, with millions of dollars' worth of NFTs being exchanged on a daily basis.

3. CryptoPunks:

CryptoPunks are a collection of 10,000 unique 24x24 pixel art characters. Each CryptoPunk is an NFT that can be owned, bought, and sold. These digital collectibles have become highly sought after, with some selling for millions of dollars. CryptoPunks are considered a groundbreaking project in the NFT space and have inspired countless other projects in the realm of digital collectibles.

4. Decentraland:

Decentraland is a virtual world built on the Ethereum blockchain, where users can buy, sell, and trade virtual land and assets. Users can create unique experiences and monetize their creations using NFTs. From virtual art galleries and casinos to virtual real estate development, Decentraland showcases the endless possibilities of NFTs in creating immersive virtual experiences.

5. Hashmasks:

Hashmasks is a collection of unique digital portraits created by a collective of artists. Each Hashmask is an NFT that can be owned and traded. The collection gained widespread popularity and has become a status symbol among collectors, with some Hashmasks selling for significant amounts that are hard to believe.

6. Bored Ape Yacht Club:

Bored Ape Yacht Club is a collection of 10,000 unique and individually hand-drawn NFT apes. Each ape comes with various traits, accessories, and attributes that make them one-of-a-kind. Owners of Bored Ape Yacht Club NFTs gain access to exclusive events and opportunities within the club, making it a highly coveted and prestigious membership in the NFT world.

7. The "Crossroads" NFT:

"Crossroads" is an NFT artwork created by musician and artist, Grimes. This piece gained attention for its unique concept and sold for a significant amount. The NFT consists of a one-minute video clip featuring various digital elements, and the ownership of the NFT grants the buyer access to an exclusive, real-life exhibition hosted by Grimes herself. This unique combination of digital art and real-life experiences highlights the potential of NFTs to bridge the gap between the virtual and physical worlds. It showcases how artists and creators can use NFTs to offer their supporters and collectors one-of-a-kind opportunities and access. The "Crossroads" NFT represents a growing trend in the NFT space, where ownership of an NFT extends beyond digital assets and into the realm of exclusive experiences.

These examples of NFTs in use today are just a glimpse into the diverse and exciting possibilities that NFTs bring to the digital world. From artwork to sports highlights to virtual land and beyond, NFTs are revolutionizing how we value and trade digital assets. As the technology and adoption of NFTs continue to evolve, it will be fascinating to see how these innovative and unique use cases further shape the future of digital ownership and creative expression.

CHAPTER 4

Trading Non-Fungible Tokens (NFTs)

As the popularity of NFTs, or non-fungible tokens, continues to soar, it's natural that more and more people are curious about how to trade in NFT. These unique digital assets are essentially one-of-a-kind, verified tokens that represent ownership of a piece of digital content such as artwork, music, and even tweets. To get started trading NFTs, there are a few key steps to take and several platforms that allow you to do so.

First, it's important to do some research and understand the basics of NFT trading. These tokens are typically created and traded on the blockchain, which is a distributed ledger technology that offers increased transparency, security, and efficiency. NFTs use a variety of different blockchain protocols such as Ethereum, EOS, and TRON, so it's important to be familiar with the platform that a specific NFT is built on.

Next, you'll need to create a digital wallet that is compatible with the blockchain platform on which you want to trade NFTs. This will allow you to store and manage your digital assets securely and enable you to interact with other participants in the NFT marketplace. Some popular digital wallets for Ethereum-based NFTs include (not limited to the following):

- **MyEtherWallet,**
- **MetaMask**, and
- **Trust Wallet**.

Once you have your digital wallet set up, you'll need to find a platform where you can buy and sell NFTs. There are several popular options, including but not limited to the following:

- **OpenSea,**
- **Rarible,**
- **SuperRare, and**
- **Nifty Gateway.**

These platforms offer a variety of different NFTs, from rare artwork and collectibles to in-game assets and virtual real estate. When you find an NFT that you're interested in purchasing, it's important to do your due diligence and ensure that it's a legitimate asset. Check the creator's reputation, verify the token's authenticity and ownership history, and make sure that you understand any restrictions or limitations associated with the asset. To trade an NFT, you'll need to place an order on a platform that supports that specific asset. Some NFTs may be sold via auction, while others may be sold at a fixed price. Once you've made a purchase, the NFT will be transferred to your digital wallet, where you can store it or resell it as desired.

It's also important to be aware of any tax implications associated with buying and selling NFTs, as these assets may be considered investments that are subject to capital gains taxes.

<u>Landmark NFT transactions includes</u>:

1. A digital artwork by artist Beeple sold for a record-breaking $69.3 million at Christie's auction house in March 2021, making it the most expensive NFT ever sold at auction.

2. The NBA has embraced digital trading cards and other collectibles to allow fans to own and trade digital versions of their favorite players' trading cards and other collectibles. In just one week in October 2020, the NBA's Top Shot platform sold $230 million.

3. Kings of Leon released their album "When You See Yourself" as an NFT in February 2021, allowing fans to purchase a digital copy of the album and exclusive bonus content and experiences.

4. Rarible, an online marketplace, has seen explosive growth in NFT sales, with more than $300 million in sales in just the first quarter of 2021.

Traditional investors and institutions have expressed interest in the NFT market, with companies such as Grayscale and CoinFund launching NFT investment funds.

In conclusion, trading NFTs can be a fun and lucrative activity for those who are willing to do their research, understand the blockchain technology behind these unique digital assets, and take the necessary steps to set up a digital wallet and find a reputable platform for buying and selling NFTs. Whether you're an art collector, gamer, or simply interested in the potential of blockchain technology, NFTs offer an exciting new way to own and trade digital assets.

CHAPTER 5

Identifying and mitigating the risk

Non-Fungible Tokens (NFTs) have been making waves in the art and entertainment world recently, with some of them fetching millions of dollars. An NFT is essentially a unique digital asset that is stored on a blockchain. The idea is that the owner of the NFT holds a verified, original version of the asset, and that this ownership can be transferred through the blockchain ledger. While the idea of NFTs is exciting, there are risks associated with their trading that must be identified and mitigated.

One of the first risks to consider with NFT trading is that of fraud. Because the NFTs exist only on the blockchain, it can be difficult to verify their authenticity. Anyone can create an NFT and put it up for sale, claiming that it is a rare or valuable asset. To mitigate this risk, it is important to only trade with reputable sellers who can provide a history of the NFT's ownership and authenticity. This means doing your research before making a purchase, checking the seller's history and verifying the NFT's authenticity through the blockchain.

Another risk associated with NFT trading is that of the technology itself. The blockchain is a relatively new and untested technology, and there are always the possibilities of technical failures or security breaches. In addition, the decentralized nature of the blockchain means that there is no central authority to manage or regulate it. To mitigate this risk, it is important to choose a trusted platform for NFT trading, one that has a proven track record of reliability and security. This platform should also have robust measures in place to protect your assets, such as encryption and multi-factor authentication.

A third risk to consider with NFT trading is that of market volatility. The value of NFTs can fluctuate wildly based on market demand,

and there is always the possibility that the value of your NFT will drop precipitously. This means that you should always be aware of the market conditions before making a purchase or sale, and that you should be prepared to hold onto your NFT for a significant period of time if necessary. Additionally, it is important to diversify your portfolio of NFTs to reduce your exposure to any one particular asset.

Finally, a fourth risk associated with NFT trading is that of regulatory uncertainty. Because the blockchain is a decentralized technology, it is often difficult to know which laws and regulations apply to it. This means that there is the possibility that governments could intervene in the market, potentially regulating or even banning the use of NFTs altogether. To mitigate this risk, it is important to stay informed of the regulatory landscape and to be aware of any legal developments that may affect NFT trading.

As with any investment, the rule is simple, **never invest more than what you are prepared to lose**. Investing in Non-Fungible Tokens (NFTs) requires traders to have access to high-speed internet connections and a stable trading platform. Trading NFTs online can be highly technical and requires a reliable internet connection and access to advanced trading tools to make informed investment decisions.

In conclusion, NFT trading is a new and exciting market that presents both opportunities and risks. While there is the potential for great rewards but also comes with several hidden risks and pitfalls, it is important to identify and mitigate the risks involved. Traders must carefully weigh the risks and rewards before entering the market and must remain vigilant about the rapidly changing conditions in this exciting, but again it will be a high-risk arena.

CHAPTER 6

Finding the right Non-Fungible Tokens (NFTs)

We all have dreams of success and greatness, but due to lack of taking action, often they remain just those dreams. To reach our highest potential, we must become action takers, not daydreamers. As an investor, you must recognize your own capabilities, and understand how to leverage your strengths. It is important to remember that being an action taker doesn't mean rushing headlong into every opportunity or task and loading your wallet with all types of Non-Fungible Tokens (NFTs), instead you must analyze and pick-up the correct NFTs for yourself. It's about having the courage, risk taking attitude, and confidence to carefully consider points before selecting the right NFTs, making wise decisions, and confidently act by contributing and purchasing your desired NFTs. You will need to carefully weigh the pros and cons of each NFTs and be willing to take risks when required, as you are aware that NFTs market is highly volatile.

Also, as an investor, you must be able to learn to verify or identify the authenticity of the NFTs before you buy it. A professional mentor can be a great source of support in this area. By having someone who has already brought different NFTs and maintains a diversified portfolio of various NFTs, can better understand your requirement ensuring that reap great returns on your investments. With the right mentor by your side, you can learn the strategy of earning profits through trading NFTs and become an action taker capable of inspiring others to learn to trade in NFTs.

This means finding a mentor who can give you the guidance and support necessary to take action and make those dreams into a reality is something that can't be ignored. A mentor will offer valuable insight and advice to help you stay on track. They can provide an outside perspective and act as a sounding board for difficult decisions. Additionally, having a mentor can help you stay motivated and focused on your goals.

Therefore, when searching for the perfect Non-Fungible Tokens (NFTs) for trading, one should first identify their investment goals. After this, research the market for potential options and pay close attention to the coin's value, market capitalization, and liquidity. Checking for updates on a NFT's technology and development can also give insights into future market performance.

Be cautious of volatile or fraudulent coins and seek advice from reputable traders or financial advisors. Additionally, consider trading on reliable exchanges and secure storage methods for purchased NFTs. Taking these steps will increase the chances of finding profitable and stable NFTs for trading.

CHAPTER 7

Investment Strategy

Investing in Non-Fungible Tokens (NFTs) is an effective way to increase one's wealth over time but remember that with great rewards comes great risks. As such, it is essential to have an ideal strategy in place that can mitigate potential losses and improve your chances of long-term gain. The best way to achieve this is by creating a diversified portfolio.

I still remember the most famous idiom, **"Don't put all your eggs in one basket."** It means, you don't risk everything by committing to one stream of investment. A variety of NFTs from various markets, geographies, asset classes, and securities make up a diversified NFTs portfolio. In addition to NFTs & Cryptocurrencies, you should think about investing in equities, bonds, commodities, and real estate. Any investor can use this method to diversify their risk and lessen the effects of any specific investment's decline.

A financial specialist or fund manager will frequently advise investors to diversify their holdings. Before constructing the optimal investment portfolio, they should consider the investor's financial objectives, risk tolerance, and personal circumstances. Keep in mind that diversification enables investors to avoid depending only on a single investment or market performance. Instead, they distribute their assets to produce a consistent and balanced return.

Additionally, diversification reduces a shareholder's losses during downturns or recessions. When the markets respond, a poorly diversified investment portfolio would see a more significant value decline. The value of a diverse portfolio would decline as well, but less so, and it would recover more quickly, keeping your investments in balance. Can you imagine a circumstance where your whole investment loses value overnight? OH NO! That could be the worst nightmare. Instead, you would be less worried about your loss in any one plan if the same money were spread across several other schemes.

Therefore, every investor should consider investment diversification to be a key guideline. Over time, it helps diversify the risk across different assets and preserves the value of your investments. Before choosing the best investment plan, building a diverse portfolio should be handled carefully and take into account a number of aspects. Investors that adhere to this approach frequently outperform their competitors and are regarded as shrewd investors. A visit to a professional investment expert or his firm would be strongly recommended to explore a wide range of investment options with your interested products.

CHAPTER 8

The Future of NFTs in the Digital World.

The future of Non-Fungible Tokens (NFTs) in the digital space is incredibly exciting and holds immense potential. As the popularity of NFTs continues to grow, we can expect to see significant advancements and new opportunities arise in the coming future.

One of the key areas of growth for NFTs is in the world of digital art. NFTs have already revolutionized the way artists monetize and protect their work, but the potential goes far beyond that. With the ability to incorporate interactive elements, virtual reality experiences, and even augmented reality, NFT art has the potential to create immersive and engaging experiences for collectors and enthusiasts. Just imagine yourself stepping into a digital art gallery and being able to explore, interact with, and even own the artworks on display and along with that you create your personal portfolio. This fusion of technology and art opens up endless possibilities for creativity and storytelling.

In addition to art, NFTs are likely to expand into other creative industries as well. Music, film, literature, and even virtual reality experiences can all be tokenized as NFTs, providing creators with new ways to distribute, monetize, and engage with their audiences. For example, musicians can release limited edition NFT albums with exclusive content or virtual reality experiences, providing fans with a truly unique and immersive way to connect with their favorite artists.

Don't forget, another area of growth for NFTs is in the world of gaming. Already, we are seeing virtual real estate and in-game items being tokenized as NFTs. This opens up new opportunities for players to truly own and trade their digital assets, creating a thriving economy within virtual worlds. As virtual reality technology continues to advance, we can expect to see even more integration between

NFTs and gaming, allowing for unique and customizable experiences for players.

Furthermore, the potential for NFTs extends beyond the creative industries. NFTs have the potential to be used for identity verification, digital ownership of physical assets, and even as a means of establishing trust and transparency in various sectors such as supply chain management and intellectual property rights which could make accessing online services more secure and less vulnerable to fraud. NFTs can also be used to establish ownership and transfer of physical assets, such as real estate and collectibles, with the added benefit of secure tracking on a blockchain. Moreover, NFTs could be utilized to ensure transparency and accuracy in areas such as supply chain management and intellectual property rights.

By tokenizing products and registering them on a blockchain, companies can track every step of the supply chain, providing transparency and reducing the risk of counterfeits. Similarly, NFTs can be used to establish ownership and protect intellectual property rights. Artists, writers, and inventors can create NFTs to prove ownership and control the use of their creations, preventing unauthorized copies or infringement. This level of security and accountability can revolutionize the way businesses operate and protect their assets.

As NFTs continue to gain traction, we can also anticipate new marketplaces and platforms dedicated to the buying, selling, and trading of these digital assets. Just as traditional art auctions have established themselves as reputable and regulated platforms, NFT marketplaces are likely to emerge as the go-to destinations for collectors and enthusiasts.

Overall, the future of NFTs in the digital space is bright. The technology has the potential to transform various industries, unlocking new possibilities for creators, providing secure and transparent transactions, and offering unique experiences for consumers. With innovation and creativity driving the growth of NFTs, it's an exciting time to be a part of the digital revolution. As more and more industries recognize the potential of NFTs, we can expect to see increased adoption and integration into everyday life. From ticketing systems to digital licenses, NFTs have the ability to streamline processes and provide enhanced security and trust.

Furthermore, as blockchain technology continues to advance and become more accessible, the barriers to entry for NFT creation and ownership will likely decrease, opening up even more opportunities for individuals and businesses alike. As with any emerging technology, there will be challenges and uncertainties along the way, but the potential rewards far outweigh the risks. The future of NFTs in the digital space is promising, and those who embrace and adapt to this new paradigm will be at the forefront of innovation and success.

CHAPTER 9

Conclusion

(With hypothetical examples)

Since its conception, the world of Non-Fungible Tokens (NFTs), has been a fascinating one. The phrase has gained in popularity over time as it continues to upend conventional finance and the way transactions are conducted. Since its inception and throughout its development in the market, Cryptocurrencies & NFTs have provided access to cutting-edge technology and the capacity to conduct transactions on a decentralized platform.

We have learnt through our conversations that blockchain technology is a decentralized method of preserving records that guarantees transactions are safe and open. It does away with the requirement for a central organization to monitor and regulate transactions. Users may conduct transactions with complete security and confidence thanks to this. We have also seen how blockchain technology has the potential to revolutionize a number of industries, including supply chain management, healthcare, and finance. Blockchain technology has made it possible for more secure, affordable, and efficient transactions with the advent of smart contracts. We have emphasized that cryptocurrencies are distinct because they control the creation of units of money and verify the flow of payments using encryption techniques. The speed, transaction costs, scalability, and security of each form of cryptocurrency are distinctive characteristics.

Additionally, we emphasized the rising acceptance of Non-Fungible Tokens (NFTs) as a form of investment, as well as how they have transformed how people see and manage money.

It is now simpler for people to invest, trade, and earn thanks to the development of multiple NFTs trading platforms. There are reputable and well-liked platforms available for traders to use while buying and selling NFTs, as we have already stated. These user-friendly platforms include a variety of tools and features that traders may use to research market trends and make wise selections. Depending on their requirements and interests, traders may choose from a number of additional trustworthy platforms than the ones mentioned above to trade NFTs. Before choosing a platform to use for trading NFTs, it is crucial to undertake adequate research to prevent losing money or falling prey to scams. Each trader is free to choose the platform that best meets their requirements and goals.

Other measures one may take to secure their money include dealing with trustworthy exchanges, employing strong passwords, and keeping a watchful eye on unusual activities. While there are always dangers associated with investments, managing them while trading cryptocurrencies is essential for anybody hoping to make money in this fascinating new market. Investors may take cautious risks in this developing market by following these measures and achieving long-term success. To sum up, selecting the correct NFTs for you might be difficult and time-consuming. But you may find the ideal fit for your requirements with a clear grasp of your investing objectives and risk tolerance, extensive study, and persistence.

Diversifying your investing portfolio is crucial to avoiding placing all of your eggs in one basket. It is advised to devote a manageable portion of your portfolio to NFTs and to regularly review your investing approach in light of the market's performance. It is important to stick to your investment strategy and not make impulsive decisions based on market fluctuations. Trying to time the market is a risky game and often leads to poor investment outcomes. A sound investment strategy allows you to weather short-term volatility and reap the benefits of long-term market growth.

Additionally, reviewing and adjusting your investment strategy periodically is also important as your circumstances and goals may change over time. By doing so, you can ensure that your investments continue to align with your overall financial objectives. A well-defined and disciplined investment strategy is a key component to successful investing. Sticking to it, despite the inevitable ups and downs of the market, can lead to better outcomes in the long run.

Lastly, a diversified investment portfolio is necessary for long-term success. Diversification helps mitigate risks associated with investing. Investors should spread their money across a range of assets classes to reduce risk. Don't forget to look for user reviews, security measures, and other important features to help ensure that you're making the best decision for your own financial future. Taking calculated risks, investing wisely, and building a diversified portfolio will lead to financial stability and a secure future.

Non-Fungible Tokens (NFTs) is a new form of investment that has its unique characteristics, which can result in significant profits or losses, depending on how well it is managed. In this chapter, we will examine five hypothetical examples showing profit and loss observed in NFT trading, they are:

1. Profit:

The first hypothetical example is about a renowned artist who recently created an NFT to sell his art. The NFT had a high level of demand as the artist's works were already popular in the market. He created an NFT for a single piece of art that sold for a whopping $500,000. The artist retained a portion of the profit as royalties. In this example, the artist made a considerable profit through the sale of the NFT.

2. Loss:

Another hypothetical example is about an NFT creator who used copyrighted materials in their NFT, leading to legal issues. The NFT was removed from the market, and the creator was sued by the copyright owner for intellectual property infringement. The lawsuit cost the creator a significant amount of money, resulting in a considerable loss in their investment.

3. Profit:

The third hypothetical example is about an NFT collector who acquired several NFTs early on, before they gained mainstream recognition. As the demand for NFTs increased, the collector sold their NFT collection at a substantial profit. The collector was able to earn a considerable return on investment in a short period, resulting in significant profit.

4. Loss:

In contrast to the previous example, this fourth hypothetical example shows the opposite effect, which is a loss due to low demand. An NFT collector purchased a rare NFT, but as time passed, demand for the NFT declined, resulting in its value decreasing. The collector eventually sold the NFT at a loss, resulting in a considerable investment loss.

5. Profit:

Lastly, the fifth hypothetical example involves the resale of NFTs. A collector bought an NFT for a moderate price, and a few months later, its demand increased due to an endorsement by a famous celebrity. The collector resold the NFT at a higher price, resulting in a significant profit. This example shows how quick buying and reselling NFTs can lead to considerable profits.

In conclusion, NFTs can result in significant profits or losses, depending on various factors, such as market demand, legal issues, and proper timing. These five hypothetical examples are not definitive but are intended to give a better understanding of how NFT trading works. Like any other form of investment, NFT trading requires proper research, due diligence, and a willingness to take calculated risks to make considerable returns.

Credits

While preparing this book some references for specific information were drawn from different websites and search engines (as noted below) like Google Search, Yahoo Search, and Wikipedia; this information was gathered solely to clarify the basic concept on this subject for my readers.

https://www.google.com

https://us.search.yahoo.com

https://en.wikipedia.org

https://www.coindesk.com

https://www.blockchain-council.org

https://cryptoslate.com

https://cointelegraph.com

https://www.pinterest.com

Thank you & Feedback.

Thank you for reading this book and following it through to the end. I hope that you enjoyed this book, and it gave you a thorough understanding of Non-Fungible Tokens (NFTs). For better results, we strongly urge you to do a self-study, analyze past performed trades, begin with investing a small amount, and please don't take impulsive decision. Then move on learning about other NFTs; after all it's you who will be investing your hard-earned money so invest wisely.

I hope you live a pleasant life filled with lots of joy & excitement and be able to create decent wealth and a diversified investment portfolio that earns you profit by producing great results on your investments. If you liked my book, I would greatly appreciate it if you could spare a moment to leave a review. Thank you for sparing your time in advance!

Warmest Regards,
S.P. Modi